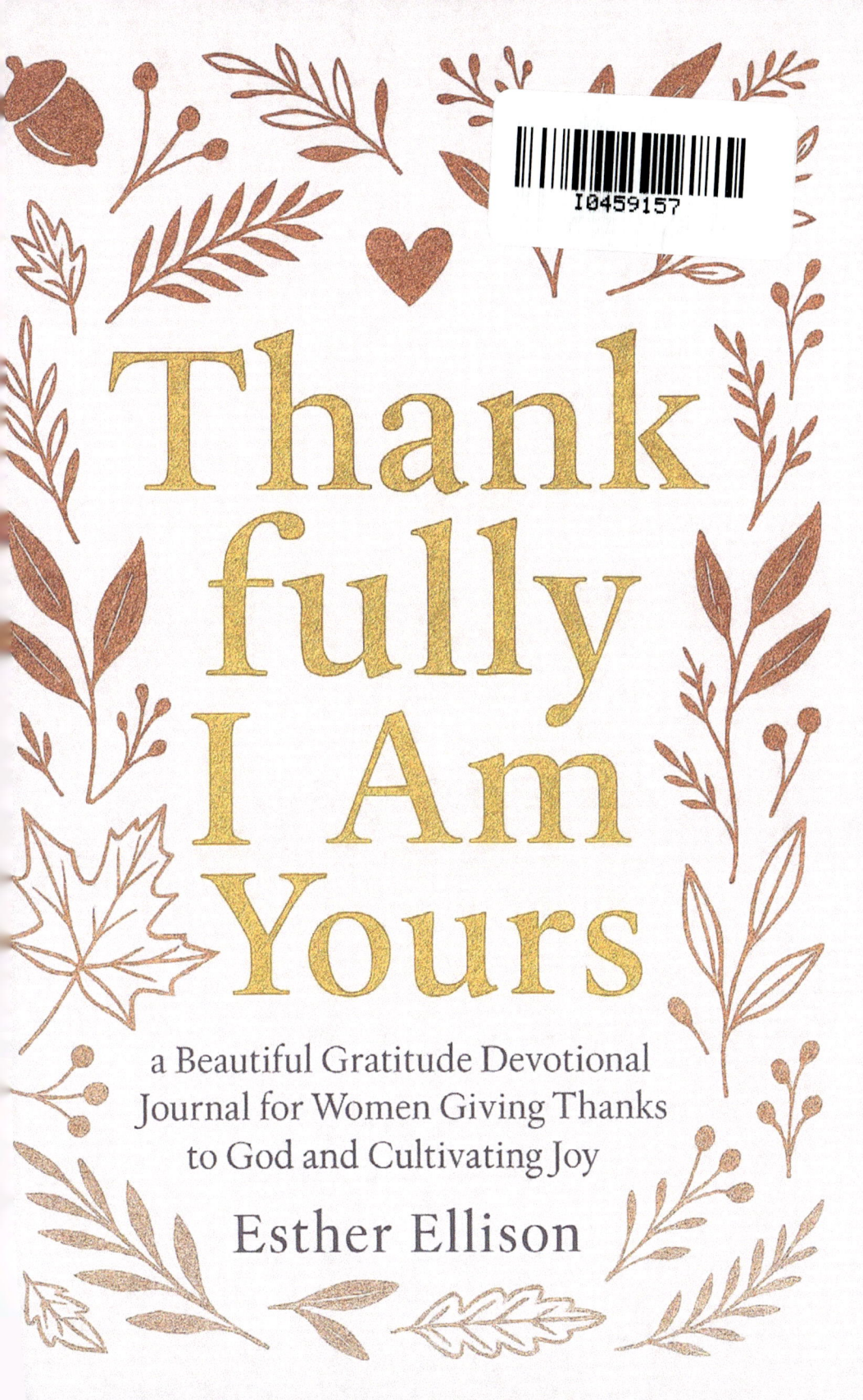

Thank fully I Am Yours

a Beautiful Gratitude Devotional
Journal for Women Giving Thanks
to God and Cultivating Joy

Esther Ellison

From:

To:

Note & Date:

_____

_____

_____

_____

_____

Table of Contents

Table of Contents

Disclaimer and Legal Notice

Finding God's Grace in Every Season

A day before Thanksgiving, our oven broke. The timing felt awful. Family was coming, the food was planned, and all I could think was, Why now, God?

I stood in the kitchen with bags of groceries and no way to cook them, fighting back frustrated tears.

Then something amazing happened. My daughter walked in carrying pies she had baked herself. Our neighbor brought over a turkey. Before I knew it, the table was full of food I hadn't even made.

The whole house smelled like cinnamon and roasted turkey. Kids were laughing and running through the rooms. Plates clinked, people talked, and prayers were whispered around the table. And for the first time, I wasn't tired or stressed. I was able to just sit, breathe, and enjoy. That day I realized Thanksgiving was never about a perfect meal. It was about being thankful for God's goodness and for the people around me.

Thankfully I Am Yours was created for women who want to live with that same kind of thankfulness. Inside you'll find:

·   Stories that sound a lot like real life, with ups and downs you can relate to.

·   Simple prayers to help when you don't know what to say.

·   Easy steps that show you how to live out your faith i n everyday ways.

As you spend time with this devotional, you'll feel more peace in your heart, more kindness with the people you love, and more joy in small, ordinary moments.

Whether someone gave this to you as a gift or you picked it up to care for your own soul, let this be a reminder of one big truth: You matter. And as you turn these pages, may you find a steady rhythm of grace.

One prayer, one step, one day at a time.

Week 1: Rooted Identity, Stable Joy

Day 1: Chosen, Not Chance

"For He chose us in Him before the creation of the world to be holy and blameless in His sight." – Ephesians 1:4

I used to think I had to earn everything, even God's love. I measured my value by how productive I was, how "spiritual" I acted, how much I pleased others. Somewhere deep down, I believed love came with conditions. Be good enough. Be strong. Be less needy. Be more impressive.

Then came the day everything unraveled. A promotion I fought hard for was given to someone else. My friendships felt strained, my prayers felt dry, and I found myself curled up in bed wondering why I felt so empty when I was doing "everything right." That's when I stumbled across Ephesians 1:4 during my quiet time.

"He chose us...before the creation of the world." Those words hit me like fresh air in a suffocating room. Chosen. Not tolerated. Not measured. Not picked for performance. Chosen before I did a single thing.

That night, I whispered through tears, "God, You really chose me?" Slowly, like dawn breaking after a long night, I felt a warmth in my soul. I started thanking Him, not for what I had done, but for what He had already done. Gratitude was not a result of my success. It was rooted in His love.

Since then, I have learned to live from being chosen, not chasing approval. When the lies of not being enough creep in, I go back to that truth. I do not have to hustle for a seat at the table. My name is already engraved on it.

Prayer

Father, thank You that I am chosen in Christ. Set my worth in what You say. Amen.

A Moment with God

Where do I still act like I must earn love, and what will I thank God for instead today?

Day 2: Beloved, Before the To-do List

"And a voice came from heaven: 'You are my Son, whom I love; with You I am well pleased.'" – Luke 3:22

I have lived many mornings with a mental checklist that shouted louder than my heart. Laundry, emails, work, kids, groceries, my worth tied to how much I accomplished. But one morning, I sat in silence before starting the day and remembered this verse. Jesus had not performed a single miracle yet, and still the Father said, *"With You I am well pleased."*

That truth gently unraveled something inside me. If the Son of God received love before He ever acted, why do I live like I must earn it? I closed my planner, sat with my coffee, and thanked God that His delight in me was not waiting at the finish line. It met me right at the start.

Now I remind myself daily: I am beloved before the to-do list begins.

Prayer

Lord, speak Your delight over me before I begin my work. Amen.

A Moment with God

What task usually defines my worth, and how will I start today loved first?

Day 3: Forgiven, Fully

"As far as the east is from the west, so far has He removed our transgressions from us." – Psalm 103:12

The shame crept in quietly. A harsh word spoken in frustration. A promise broken. A failure I replayed on loop in my mind.

I kept asking God to forgive me, but peace did not come. That is when I realized I was not doubting God's mercy, I was doubting He really gave it to me.

Psalm 103:12 reminded me: when God forgives, He removes. He does not hold it in reserve, waiting to throw it back in my face. It is gone. Really gone.

I knelt and said out loud, "Thank You for forgiving me, fully. Help me live like it is true." Gratitude began to rise. Not just for what I had been freed from, but for who I was becoming because of His grace.

Prayer

Jesus, thank You for removing my guilt. Teach me to live forgiven. Amen.

A Moment with God

What guilt do I carry that You have already lifted?

Day 4: Fearfully and Wonderfully Made

"I praise You because I am fearfully and wonderfully made; Your works are wonderful, I know that full well." – Psalm 139:14

I used to stand in front of the mirror and critique everything I saw. Too soft. Too round. Not enough here. Too much there.

Even though I praised God with my mouth, I tore down His creation in my mind. Then one morning, I read Psalm 139 again, not skimming, but slowly.

"Fearfully and wonderfully made." My body was not a problem to fix. It was a gift, crafted with intention.

That day, I started thanking God for what my body did, not just how it looked. Lungs that breathe without instruction. Legs that carry me. A heart that beats with resilience. Gratitude healed the comparison.

The more I thanked Him, the less I criticized myself.

Prayer

Creator, thank You for my body's design. Help me bless it, not belittle it. Amen.

A Moment with God

Name three functions of your body you are grateful for today.

Day 5: Renewed Mind, New Lens

"Do not conform to the pattern of this world, but be transformed by the renewing of your mind." – Romans 12:2

My thoughts used to spiral quickly. One small disappointment would turn into, "I am failing again. I will never get it right." Gratitude disappeared, buried beneath lies I did not even realize I was believing.

Then I learned this truth: the mind is a battlefield. God's Word is the weapon. Romans 12:2 gave me permission to trade in my toxic patterns for truth.

So I started catching those thoughts. Replacing "I am failing" with "I am learning." Swapping "I will never change" with "God is still working on me."

Gratitude came not because everything was perfect, but because my perspective changed. A renewed mind does not wait for better circumstances. It sees them differently.

Prayer

Spirit, renew my mind and reset my focus to what is good. Amen.

A Moment with God

Which repeated thought needs renewing, and what true thought will replace it?

Your feedback is a true blessing!

If this book has encouraged you or helped you feel less alone, would you leave a quick review?

Even one sentence makes a huge difference and takes just a minute. As a small author, your feedback not only lifts my heart... It also helps other women of faith find the support and hope they need.

Thank you for being part of this journey!

Scan this QR code with your phone to go to the review page

Or

Go to your orders, find the book and click

"Write a product review"

Thank you <3

Week 2: Quieting Anxiety and Overwhelm

Day 6: Peace That Guards

"Do not be anxious about anything, but in every situation, by prayer and petition, with thanksgiving, present your requests to God. And the peace of God, which transcends all understanding, will guard your hearts and your minds in Christ Jesus." – Philippians 4:6–7

The night felt endless. My thoughts ran in circles. What if the bill is late? What if the meeting tomorrow goes wrong? What if I let everyone down?

I prayed, but it sounded more like begging than believing. That is when I noticed something in Philippians I had skimmed past before: **with thanksgiving.** I had been handing God my worries but forgetting to add gratitude.

So I tried it: "God, I am worried about the bills, but thank You that You have never left me hungry." "I am stressed about tomorrow's meeting, but thank You that You have given me the skills I need." "I feel like I will fail, but thank You that Your love for me is not based on success."

Something shifted. The circumstances did not change, but my chest loosened. It was like God placed a shield around my mind. Gratitude did not erase the storm, but it kept the storm from erasing me.

Now when anxiety rises, I picture peace as a guard at my door. Thanksgiving is the key that lets Him in.

Prayer

God, I bring my worries with thanks. Guard my heart and mind. Amen.

A Moment with God

List three worries and write one sentence of thanks beside each.

Day 7: Daily Bread, Not Tomorrow's

"Therefore do not worry about tomorrow, for tomorrow will worry about itself. Each day has enough trouble of its own." – Matthew 6:34

I once carried an invisible backpack filled with "what ifs." What if I lose the job? What if my kids struggle? What if the future does not turn out the way I hope?

By noon, the weight of tomorrow was crushing me today. Jesus pointed me back to the present. "Pray for daily bread." Not a lifetime supply. Just today's portion.

When I started thanking Him for today—the food on the table, the phone call I could return, the laughter I almost missed—I realized how often I was living in days that had not even arrived yet.

Gratitude does not erase the future, but it keeps me from dragging it into today. My soul breathes easier when I let God handle tomorrow and simply receive the bread He has placed in my hands right now.

Prayer

Father, help me receive today's portion and release the rest. Amen.

A Moment with God

What future burden will I set down for 24 hours?

Day 8: Light for the Next Step

"Your word is a lamp for my feet, a light on my path." – Psalm 119:105

ne night, I lost power at home. With only a small flashlight in hand, I realized I could see enough for one step, not the whole room. It struck me that this is how God guides.

I want the floodlights, the ten-year plan, the assurance of outcomes. But God gives step–light, not spotlight. Enough for the next obedient move.

Gratitude helps me accept that gift. Instead of panicking over what I do not know, I thank Him for the clarity I do have. A verse that speaks. A nudge to call a friend. The wisdom to rest instead of push.

Step by step, light by light, He leads me. Looking back, I see that every single step was enough.

Prayer

Lord, thank You for the next clear step. I will walk in it. Amen.

A Moment with God

What is the next faithful step, not the next ten?

Day 9: The Yoke That Fits

"Come to Me, all you who are weary and burdened, and I will give you rest... For My yoke is easy and My burden is light." – Matthew 11:28–30

I was carrying too much. Unrealistic expectations. People-pleasing. The endless drive to prove myself.

The more I tried to juggle, the heavier it felt. One day, reading this passage, I saw Jesus was not inviting me to add Him on top of my load. He was inviting me to exchange it.

A yoke is meant to fit. His is not crushing. It is gentle. It does not demand perfection. It walks with me in grace.

When I began thanking Him for small pockets of rest...a nap, a slow meal, a laugh, I realized gratitude is what loosens the grip of strain. Peace grows when I lay down the yoke I picked up and slip into the one He actually made for me.

Prayer

Jesus, I exchange my strain for Your rest. Amen.

A Moment with God

Which expectation feels heavy, and how will I adjust it to fit grace?

Day 10: He Gives Sleep

"In vain you rise early and stay up late, toiling for food to eat, for He grants sleep to those He loves." – Psalm 127:2

I used to treat rest like a reward, something I earned after I worked hard enough. But no matter how much I pushed, sleep did not come easily. My mind replayed the day, racing into tomorrow.

Then Psalm 127 reminded me that sleep is a gift. God does not wait until I have achieved enough to hand it over. He gives it because He loves me.

So I started ending my nights with gratitude. "Thank You for this bed. Thank You for carrying what I cannot finish. Thank You that the world will keep spinning while I rest." That simple shift unclenched my mind.

Rest became holy, not guilty. Gratitude prepares the heart for sleep, reminding us that God never slumbers, so we can.

Prayer

Giver of rest, teach me to lie down in peace. Amen.

A Moment with God

One boundary I will set tonight to protect sleep.

Week 3: Warm Relationships

Day 11: Blessing Your Spouse

"He who finds a wife finds what is good and receives favor from the Lord." – Proverbs 18:22

We were both tired. The kitchen was a mess, and the dishwasher blinked an error like it was mocking us. He loaded dishes the "wrong" way, and I pointed it out. Then I pointed out two more things. His shoulders sank. He did not say much, but the air felt heavy.

I went to the bedroom and opened my Bible to cool off. My eyes fell on Proverbs 18:22. I had read it before, but that night it spoke in a new way. A spouse is not a project. A spouse is favor. If God calls him a gift, why do I act like a critic?

I sat on the edge of the bed and thought about our early years. The jokes we shared. The way he brings me tea without asking. The way he steadies me when I spiral. Somewhere along the way I had become a fault finder. Gratitude shifts everything. It moves me from fault finding to gift finding.

I went back to the kitchen and tried again. "Thank you for doing the dishes," I said, honestly. "I saw you jump in when I was tired. I appreciate that." He looked up, surprised, and smiled a little. The heaviness lifted.

The next week, I put a sticky note on the coffee container: "Thanks for how you care for us." I made a list in my phone of three things I love about him. When I felt the urge to correct, I paused and asked God to soften my tone. A gentle word made space for laughter again.

Gratitude did not make us perfect, but it changed my sight. I began to see him as a person to bless, not a problem to fix. Favor, right in my own house.

Prayer

Lord, show me my spouse as a gift. Soften my tone today. Amen.

A Moment with God

List three qualities you appreciate in your spouse and one way to express thanks.

Day 12: Children as Heritage

"Children are a heritage from the Lord, offspring a reward from Him." – Psalm 127:3

The morning was loud. Cereal spilled. Shoes were missing. Someone cried because their sock "felt weird," and I felt my patience leaking out. I wanted quiet. I wanted order. I wanted five minutes to drink my coffee while it was still hot.

As I wiped the counter, Psalm 127 came to mind. A heritage. A reward. Not a setback. Not a burden. I looked up and saw it differently. The noise was not proof that I was failing. It was proof that life was here. Growth is messy. Joy can be sticky.

I took a slow breath and thanked God out loud, even while stepping over backpacks. "Thank You for these little lives. Thank You for their curiosity and their strong opinions. Thank You that I get to be here."

Something softened. Instead of snapping, I knelt and helped tie the shoe. I lingered for a six-second hug and breathed in their hair that smelled like shampoo and syrup. We laughed at the sock drama and found a pair that felt "just right."

That afternoon, I started a simple habit. I chose one moment to savor with each child. Eye contact while they told a long story. A high five over a tiny victory. A note in a lunchbox. Gratitude reframed the noise. It became music, not chaos. It reminded me that this season will pass, and I will miss the little hands, the little shoes, the little voices calling my name.

No day is perfect, but I no longer measure it by how quiet it is. I measure it by how present I am. Heritage lives here. Reward lives here. Gratitude helps me see it.

Prayer

Father, thank You for these lives entrusted to me. Amen.

A Moment with God

What moment with a child can I savor today?

Day 13: Friendship that Sharpens

"As iron sharpens iron, so one person sharpens another." – Proverbs 27:17

I got a message from a close friend after a tough meeting. "Can I share something hard with you?" My stomach flipped. I wanted praise, not feedback. But I said yes.

She spoke with care. "I noticed you shut down when you felt challenged. I think your voice matters, but fear made you pull back." It stung. Not because she was harsh, but because she was right.

I wanted to defend myself. Instead, I paused. I remembered Proverbs 27:17. Iron on iron makes sparks, but it also makes a blade that can cut true. I whispered a quick prayer. "God, help me receive this as a gift."

Then I said the words I needed to say. "Thank you for telling me the truth. I know you love me." Gratitude honored her courage. It opened my ears.

That week I asked her to check in with me before a big presentation. We practiced answers. She reminded me to breathe and speak up. I texted her after and thanked her for sharpening me. She texted back, "That is what friends do."

Gratitude helps me treasure friends who refine me instead of running from the discomfort. It also calls me higher as a friend. I want to be the one who gives courage, not just comfort. The one who celebrates wins and also points out the spinach in your teeth before you go on stage.

Sharpening is not about being harsh. It is about being honest with kindness. It is about standing close, holding up a mirror, and believing the best. Thank God for friends like that. May I be one too.

Prayer

God, help me be the kind of friend who gives courage. Amen.

A Moment with God

Which friend needs a word of thanks from me today?

Day 14: Gentle Answer in Conflict

"A gentle answer turns away wrath, but a harsh word stirs up anger." – Proverbs 15:1

The text came in hot. Short sentences. Sharp edges. My heart sped up, and I drafted a comeback that would prove my point. I wanted to win. I wanted to be right.

Then this proverb surfaced in my mind like a lifeline. A gentle answer turns away wrath. Not silence that avoids truth. Gentleness that tells the truth with a soft edge.

I put my phone down and took three deep breaths. I thanked God for something true about the other person, even if I was upset. "Thank You for their passion. Thank You that we both care." Gratitude cooled my anger and opened my ears.

I tried again. "I hear you. I want to understand. Can we talk for five minutes so we do not read tone into texts?" The call helped. We named the real issue. We both apologized. We found a solution we could both live with.

Since then, I keep a small plan for conflict. First, pause. Pray thanks for at least one true thing about the person or the goal. Second, pick gentleness on purpose. Use phrases like "Help me understand" and "Here is how I experienced it." Third, choose repair over being right. Say the hard thing with a soft voice.

Gentleness is not weakness. It is strength under control. Gratitude makes it possible. It reminds me that people are not problems. They are image bearers. A gentle answer will not fix every fight, but it often opens a door that a harsh word would slam shut.

Prayer

Spirit, place gentleness on my tongue. Amen.

A Moment with God

Identify a recent conflict. What grateful truth could have softened it?

Day 15: Boundaries that Bless

"For each one should carry their own load." – Galatians 6:5

There was a stretch of months when I said yes to everything. Extra shifts. Committees. Last minute favors. I told myself it was loving. Then resentment crept in. I snapped at my family. I felt empty and angry. Love was leaking out because I had no limits.

Galatians 6:5 helped me sort things out. There are loads I am meant to carry and loads others are meant to carry. Boundaries protect love. They help me serve from a full heart, not from guilt.

I started small. I wrote my top three priorities for the week and blessed them in prayer. I practiced a kind no. "Thank you for asking. I cannot take that on right now." I set one simple boundary for evenings: no work emails after dinner. At first it felt selfish. Then I noticed something. Peace returned. My yes grew stronger because it was honest.

Gratitude played a key part. I thanked God for my limits. I thanked Him for the people He placed around me who could step up when I could not. I thanked Him for rest that makes me more present. The more I thanked Him, the less guilty I felt about healthy limits.

Boundaries are not walls to keep people out. They are gates that help love flow in the right way. They make space for joy to grow. They keep bitterness low. They remind me that I am human, and that is good.

Prayer

Lord, guide my yes and my no. Amen.

A Moment with God

Where do I need a boundary to protect peace this week?

Week 4: Faithful Work, Grateful Heart

Day 16: Work Unto the Lord

"Whatever you do, work at it with all your heart, as working for the Lord, not for people." – Colossians 3:23

The sink was a mountain of plates, the inbox was louder than a crowd, and the laundry basket kept giving me looks. I moved from chore to chore with a tight jaw and a tired heart. I thought real ministry was the Bible study I would lead later, or the thing with a platform and applause. This was just... dishes.

Halfway through scrubbing a pan, the verse came to mind. Whatever you do. Not only the things that get noticed. Not only the tasks that match my title or my dreams.Whatever. If I do it for the Lord, it becomes worship, not just work. So I tried something simple. I whispered, "This is for You," and named the task. Folding towels became a quiet thank You for warm showers and a family to dry off. Answering emails became an act of service for people who needed my help. Cooking dinner turned into praise for the hands that could stir and the mouths that would be fed. I turned on a worship playlist and matched my pace to the music, not the pressure. The kitchen did not glow, the inbox did not disappear, yet my heart softened.

Gratitude changed the room. Motivation without burnout started to look ordinary. I set a timer for focused work, then took a small break to breathe and pray. I asked myself, who does this serve, and how does it love them well. That question anchored me to purpose. When I caught myself grumbling, I practiced a quick swap. Thank You for the meal we already have. Thank You for a job that pays the light bill. Thank You for the chance to show love in small ways. By the time the last dish clinked into the rack, I felt lighter. Nothing fancy, just faithful. Worship had been hiding in plain sight, right between the sponge and the subject line. Gratitude opened the door and invited Jesus into the grind.

Prayer

Jesus, meet me in my work today. Take my lists, my chores, my deadlines, and make them holy in Your hands. Teach me to serve with joy, to notice the people my work blesses, and to offer each task to You with a grateful heart. Amen.

A Moment with God

Choose one task and write how it serves someone you love.

Day 17: Wisdom for Decisions

"If any of you lacks wisdom, you should ask God, who gives generously to all without finding fault, and it will be given." – James 1:5

I stared at two open tabs on my laptop. One was a job posting that promised growth. The other was my current schedule, already packed. My mind spun with what ifs.

What if I pick wrong. What if I miss God's will. The pressure made me freeze. James says to ask.Not beg, not bargain, ask. And trust that God gives generously. Gratitude expects a generous God, so I started with thanks. Thank You for choices.

Thank You that You speak. Thank You that Your wisdom is not a secret code. I made a simple plan. First, pray and ask directly.Lord, I need wisdom. Speak in a way I will not miss. Second, open the Bible and listen. I read Proverbs slowly and underlined what matched this decision.

Third, invite counsel. I called two people who knew both my strengths and my limits, and I asked them to be honest. Fourth, take one small step to test the path, not a leap off a cliff. The step was an informational call about the new role.

As I listened, I felt a quiet check in my spirit about the timing. It was not fear, it was clarity. Meanwhile, my current work had doors opening that matched my gifts. The pressure lifted.Wisdom was not a lightning strike; it was a path that got brighter as I walked. I wrote down what I heard to fight the urge to second guess. I thanked God again, not because I had every detail, but because He was guiding me. Gratitude kept my heart soft and my ears open.

The decision did not make me a hero. It made me a daughter who trusted her Father to lead.

Prayer

God, I ask for wisdom, and I thank You for it. Guard my mind from fear and hurry. Help me hear Your voice through Scripture, wise counsel, and steady steps. Give me courage to obey the light I have today, and peace to wait for what I do not yet see. Amen.

A Moment with God

What decision needs wisdom, and what is my first step to seek it?

Day 18: Contentment Map

"Godliness with contentment is great gain." – 1 Timothy 6:6

Scrolling took five minutes and stole my peace for hours. New kitchens, new clothes, new trips. My heart kept whispering, if I had that, I would be happy. My budget and my spirit both felt thin.

Then this verse landed in my chest. Contentment is not a downgrade. It is a gain. So I drew a map.

In the center, I wrote, "Enough." Around it, I wrote the areas that felt loud: home, wardrobe, tech, schedule, food. For each one, I asked, what is enough for this season. Not forever, not for my neighbor, for me, right now. Home enough was clear counters and a clean table, not a remodel. Wardrobe enough was six outfits I love and wear, not a haul. Tech enough was a phone that works and screen limits after dinner. Schedule enough was one night a week open. Food enough was simple meals that feed real people. Naming enough settled me. Gratitude flowed where comparison had dried me out. I started to notice what I already had. The soft sweatshirt I reach for. The dented pan that makes the best roasted chicken. The couch where we laugh. Contentment made room for joy. To practice, I set two guardrails. First, a 24 hour pause before buying anything that promised a new life. Second, a weekly pantry check to use what we have. I unsubscribed from three email lists that poked at my wants. I also picked one area to lean into enough this week. I chose my closet. I made a tiny capsule and boxed the rest for thirty days. Freedom felt like space on a rod. Contentment is not quitting desire. It is training desire to serve what matters. Godliness with contentment is gain you can feel in your chest, like a deep breath that finally lands. Enough is a gift, and it is already here.

Prayer

Father, teach me the gain of enough. Quiet the noise of comparison and hurry. Show me where I already have more than I notice, and help me enjoy it with gratitude. Lead me to simple choices that honor You, love people, and free my heart to rest. Amen.

A Moment with God

Name one area to practice "enough" this week.

Day 19: Creativity as Image Bearing

"He has filled them with skill to do all kinds of work... all of them skilled workers and designers." – Exodus 35:35

I sat at my desk with a blank page and a nervous stomach. A new project needed a fresh idea, and I felt ordinary. Then I remembered Bezalel and Oholiab, artisans filled by God for the work. Creativity is not a club for a few.It is part of bearing God's image, given for service. I prayed, Creator, You make beauty and order. Fill me for this. Then I set small, kind limits to spark ideas. Ten minutes, one clear problem, three rough drafts. I stopped waiting for perfect and aimed for helpful. I thought about the people this work would serve and pictured their faces. That shifted my goal from impress to bless.The first draft was clunky. The second had a spark. The third made me smile. I shared it with a teammate and asked for honest feedback. We shaped it together until it worked. When the idea landed in our meeting, it did not get applause. It got results, and a thank you from someone who found their job easier because of it. That was worship. To keep creating, I started a small rhythm. I collect sparks in a notes app, things I notice at the store, on a walk, during a conversation. I practice a daily five minute doodle of ideas for my work, even if I never use them. I try one small creative risk each week, like pitching a new format or testing a different process.

Not reckless, just brave enough to grow. Creativity is not about being loud. It is about being generous with the gifts God put in your hands. When I show up with gratitude, the pressure to be original melts.I am not making my name; I am carrying His heart into my work.

Prayer

Creator, breathe fresh ideas into my work. Fill my hands and mind with skill that serves people well. Free me from fear of failure and from pride that tries to impress. Make my creativity a channel of Your love, order, and beauty in the everyday. Amen.

A Moment with God

What small creative risk will I take in my calling?

Day 20: Sabbath Prep

"The Sabbath was made for people, not people for the Sabbath." – Mark 2:27

Our Sundays were a scramble. Half-finished chores, forgotten groceries, and naps that never happened. I kept saying rest mattered, but I treated it like a surprise party I did not plan. No wonder it never showed up.

Jesus said the Sabbath was made for us, a gift that needs intention. I tried a simple shift. Prepare like rest is coming. On Friday night, I made a short list labeled Sabbath Prep.

Two loads of laundry, clear the table, quick grocery run for easy meals, set out the Bible and a candle. I asked the family to help. Ten minutes of tidying together changed the feel of the house. On Saturday morning, I cooked double for dinner so Sunday could be heat and eat.

I put my phone in a basket by the door with a note to myself, you are not needed by everyone today. I set an away message on email that said I would answer on Monday. I picked one anchor for joy, a slow walk after church or a puzzle at the table. When Sunday came, we were not perfect, but we were ready.

We lingered at breakfast without staring at a pile of chores. I read a Psalm and took a nap without guilt. When my mind reached for work, I told it, not today, and returned to the gift in front of me. By evening, I felt full instead of empty. The week ahead still had challenges, yet my soul felt steady. Rest does not happen by accident. It grows where we guard it. Sabbath does not demand fancy rules.It invites a posture of trust that God keeps the world while I stop. That trust is hard and holy. Gratitude helps. Thank You for a body that needs sleep.

Thank You for a day without striving. Thank You that my worth is not my output.

Prayer

Lord of the Sabbath, help me prepare to truly rest. Teach me to finish what must be done and release what can wait. Meet me in the quiet, renew my mind, and refresh my body. Let my rest say loudly, I trust You with all I cannot control. Amen.

A Moment with God

What two tasks will I finish early to guard rest this week?

Week 5: Embodied Grace

Day 21: Food as Provision

"Give us today our daily bread." – Matthew 6:11

The grocery aisle felt like a test. I stared at labels the way a lawyer studies a contract, hunting for hidden traps. Sugar here. Oil there.

My cart held the "safe" foods, but my chest felt tight. By the time I got home, fear had set the mood for dinner. I cooked chicken and a bright salad, but the table felt tense. My daughter asked, "Can we have bread with this?"

My mouth said, "Not tonight." My heart said, We do not have room. It was not just about carbs. It was about control.

It was the old fear that there would not be enough, not enough food, not enough willpower, not enough of me. That fear had roots. I remembered the pantry from my childhood, sometimes full, sometimes not. I remembered the first diet I tried, the praise I got for saying no, the way I learned to argue with my own hunger.

Somewhere along the way, eating became a battlefield. Peace did not live at my table. After we cleared the plates, I stood by the sink and whispered the Lord's Prayer. When I reached, "Give us today our daily bread," it landed differently.

Not my monthly plan. Not tomorrow's control. Today's bread. Today's care.

As if on cue, our neighbor knocked with a pot of soup and a small bag of warm rolls. "We made extra," she smiled. I almost said, "We are fine," but something softer rose up. I set the soup on the stove, tore a roll in half, and breathed in the steam.

I prayed, "Thank You for daily bread." We sat again. We ate slowly. The soup was simple and good.

The roll was soft. My daughter laughed, and the room loosened. The fear that had been gripping my shoulders let go. Gratitude changed the room before the food changed my body.

That night, I wrote one sentence and taped it to the fridge: Gratitude removes fear from the table. It became my small rule of life. Before I eat, I thank God. I plan one simple meal that brings peace, not pressure.

I sit down, chew, and listen to my body. I stop when satisfied. I keep space for joy. I buy the bread and share it.

I trust that the One who fed Israel in a desert and Elijah under a tree can

care for my kitchen today.

Prayer

Provider, thank You for today's bread. Teach my heart to trust You for enough. Quiet fear that makes me hoard, restrict, or rush. Help me receive food as a gift, eat with peace, stop when satisfied, and share gladly with others today. Keep my table filled with gratitude always. Amen.

A Moment with God

One simple meal plan choice that serves peace today.

Day 22: Movement as Praise

"Let everything that has breath praise the Lord. Praise the Lord." – Psalm 150:6

I used to think movement had to hurt to count. If I ate a cupcake, I felt I owed the treadmill. I kept score in my head, and exercise became a payment plan that never ended. No wonder I quit again and again.

Who wants to show up for punishment? One morning, I woke early. The house was quiet, the sky still gray. I stood in the kitchen rubbing sleep from my eyes and felt the smallest nudge: what if you moved for joy, not payback?

I put on a song that makes me smile and shuffled in my old leggings. The beat found my feet. I swayed, then spun, then laughed at myself. Ten minutes later, I was warm, not weary.

The verse came to mind, "Let everything that has breath praise the Lord." I felt my breath in my chest like a drum. Praise did not need a gym. It needed a willing body and a thankful heart.

I walked outside and let the cool air touch my face. The birds were already singing. I joined them with my steps. That day, I made a quiet switch.

I stopped asking, How many calories will this burn? I started asking, How can my breath praise God right now? Some days it looked like a 10-minute walk while dinner simmered. Some days it was stretching on the floor while my son built towers.

Some days it was dancing in the kitchen, wooden spoon as a microphone. Movement became celebration, not punishment. The surprise was how my body responded to kindness. I wanted to move more because I no longer feared the scorecard.

I slept better. My moods softened. My joints thanked me. The joy did not come from perfect form.

It came from presence. Every step said, I am alive, and God is good. If movement has felt like a judge's gavel, let this be your permission slip. Put on a song.

Walk around the block. Breathe out stress. Breathe in praise. Ten minutes can turn your whole day.

Prayer

Lord, I will praise You with breath and steps. Turn my movement into celebration, not payback. Guard me from shame. Fill my lungs with joy, my joints with ease, my mind with song. Let ten minutes of motion become worship that lifts my heart toward You, Giver of life. Amen.

A Moment with God

What 10-minute movement will I enjoy today?

Day 23: Body Image and Blessing

"You are not your own; you were bought at a price. Therefore honor God with your bodies." – 1 Corinthians 6:19–20

The mirror in the fitting room was unfair. The lights were bright and close, and my thoughts turned sharp. My eyes went to the places I have trained them to go. My stomach.

My thighs. I tugged at the fabric and heard the old chorus: Not enough here. Too much there. I wanted to hide.

I also wanted to fight. I stood still and prayed one line, "Lord, is there another way to see?" The verse surfaced, steady and gentle. My body is a temple of the Holy Spirit.

Not a project. Not a trend. A place for God to dwell. The word temple changed the room.

Temples are not judged like billboards. They are tended. They are honored. I thought of my friend who is recovering from surgery, the way she smiles at every breath like it is a gift.

I thought of the hands that hold my child's face when he cries, hands that belong to this body I speak so harshly to. Right there, I wrote a blessing under my breath. "Thighs, thank you for carrying me to work, to the park, to the altar on my wedding day. Belly, thank you for holding laughter and lunches and the deep inhale I take when I am overwhelmed.

Arms, thank you for hugging, lifting, worshiping." My reflection did not change shape. My posture did. Blessing moved me from critique to care.

Stewardship is different from obsession. It looks like feeding my body decent food. It looks like choosing clothes that fit now, not punishing myself with sizes that ache. It looks like fresh air and water and sleep.

It looks like gratitude that this body, with its stories and scars, lets me live and love. I bought a swimsuit that felt good when I moved. I walked out of the store lighter. Not because I fixed myself, but because I blessed what God has claimed.

My worth is not measured in mirrors. It is anchored in a price already paid.

Prayer

Spirit, teach me to honor my body with gratitude. Silence the harsh critic. Help me bless what I usually hide, and treat this temple with care. Guide my choices toward nourishment, clothing that fits now, and gentle rest. Let your love reshape my view until I see sacred design. Amen.

A Moment with God

Write a blessing over a part of your body you often critique.

Day 24: Strength in Weakness

"My grace is sufficient for you, for my power is made perfect in weakness." – 2 Corinthians 12:9

I woke with a headache that felt like a drum. My to-do list did not care. Emails. Carpool.

Dinner. A workout I had promised myself I would not skip. I told my body, "We are doing this," and pushed into the day like a soldier. By noon, I was shaky and snappy.

My son asked a simple question, and I snapped like a dry twig. I saw the look on his face and felt the truth hit. I was running on fumes and pride. I did not want to need help.

I wanted to be the one who could do it all. The verse came to mind like a hand on my shoulder. "My grace is sufficient for you." I sat on the edge of the bed and let the words settle.

What if weakness is not failure but a doorway? What if asking for help is holy? I texted a friend, "Headache will not quit. Can you grab the kids?"

She replied in minutes, "Yes." I ordered takeout instead of forcing myself to cook. I closed my eyes for twenty minutes and let the room be quiet. The world kept spinning.

No one fired me from motherhood. The sky did not fall. When I woke, the pain had softened. More than that, the pressure had lifted.

I felt small and held, like a child who finally stops fighting sleep. Strength met me, but not the kind I was trying to manufacture. It was borrowed. It was given.

It was grace. Since then, I look for the place I can ask instead of push. Can the kids fold their laundry? Can I swap favors with a friend?

Can I choose one priority instead of five? My limits are not walls to bang my head against. They are signposts pointing to God's power.

Prayer

Jesus, I receive Your strength in my weakness. I lay down hurry and pride. Meet my limits with grace. Show me where to ask for help, and whom to call. Put peace in my pace. Power me to choose less, love more, and rest inside Your care today, please. Amen.

A Moment with God

Where will I ask for help today rather than push through?

Day 25: Sleep, Sunlight, and Simple Care

"Get up and eat, for the journey is too much for you." – 1 Kings 19:7–8

I cried on the kitchen floor over a sink of dishes. Nothing dramatic had happened. It was the slow drain of many days. Late nights. Early alarms. Coffee for breakfast. Scrolling instead of rest. I kept telling myself, "Be stronger," but my body kept telling the truth.

I remembered Elijah under the broom tree, done with everything. God did not give him a speech. An angel touched him and said, "Get up and eat." Then he slept again.

Then he ate again. Only after that did he move on. Sometimes the most spiritual thing is a nap and a snack. So I tried it.

I set a timer for twenty minutes and closed my eyes. I put my phone in another room. When the timer chimed, I scrambled an egg, toasted bread, and ate at the table with a glass of water. Then I stepped onto the porch and let the sun warm my face.

My shoulders dropped like a load had been taken. Those thirty minutes did not fix my week, but they changed the way I faced it. I felt cared for instead of scolded. I realized I had been asking my soul to run a marathon with no fuel.

God was not mad at me for needing rest. He was meeting me with it. Now I look for small upgrades that honor my humanity. I set a gentle bedtime and keep it.

I put a cup by the sink and drink water when I enter the kitchen. I open the curtains when I wake and step into morning light for a few breaths. Simple care is not selfish. It is stewardship.

When we treat our bodies like enemies, everything gets harder. When we treat them like gifts, our gratitude grows. Sleep, sunlight, and simple meals become testimonies. They say, God made me.

God sustains me. God will carry me through this day.

Prayer

Shepherd, lead me into simple care without guilt. Help me notice hunger, fatigue, and daylight as gifts from You. Remind me to sleep, to eat, to

drink water, and to step outside. Renew me through small habits that heal my heart and mind for tomorrow's work and joy today. Amen.

A Moment with God

Which basic habit needs one small upgrade this week?

Week 6: Little Foxes, Small Habits, Big Joy

Day 26: Taming the Scroll

"Teach us to number our days, that we may gain a heart of wisdom." Psalm 90:12

My thumb had a mind of its own. Before my feet hit the floor, I opened my phone, checked three apps, skimmed a headline that raised my blood pressure, and fell into a reel of home makeovers I could not afford. Twenty minutes vanished. Breakfast was rushed, my tone was sharp, and my heart was tired before 8 a.m.

Later, while standing in the kitchen hunting for my missing keys and my peace, Psalm 90:12 floated up like a gentle nudge. Number your days. I counted what I had already spent. Twenty minutes of life traded for noise.

I pictured my day as a jar of marbles, each marble a moment I could spend with God, my family, or on work that mattered. I realized I had poured a handful down the drain of notifications. That night I tried something simple. I charged my phone in the kitchen, not by my bed.

I set my alarm on a tiny clock and promised God the first fifteen minutes. The next morning, my hand still reached for the phone that was not there. I laughed at myself, made tea, opened my Bible, and breathed. The house was quiet, my mind was clear, and when my daughter wandered in, we had time to scramble eggs slowly.

No rushing. No snapping. I felt like I had traded static for a song. The day still had noise, but it did not own me.

I added two more boundaries. First, no phone at the table. Second, a thirty minute block in the afternoon for texts and updates so I was not nibbling all day. I even switched my screen to grayscale.

The bright colors had been bait. Gray made it boring in the best way. By evening, I noticed something small and holy. I remembered faces from conversations.

I did not walk into rooms and forget why. My mind felt less crowded. The verse was right. Wisdom grows when I count what matters most.

Number your days, not your notifications. Phones are tools, not tyrants. When I put them in their place, joy has room to sit at the table.

Prayer

Lord, teach me wise time. Train my hands to reach for Your presence before my phone. Help me set simple, strong boundaries that serve my soul and my people. Fill my day with focus, gentle pace, and clear choices that honor You. Amen.

A Moment with God

What phone boundary will I practice for 24 hours?

Day 27: Interruptions as Invitations

"Jesus, aware that power had gone out from him, stopped and said, 'Who touched me?'" Mark 5:30–34

I planned the day like a puzzle, every piece tight. Groceries at nine. Emails by ten. A quick workout.

Then my neighbor knocked with a bag of lemons and a heavy story. My body stayed at the door, but my mind tapped its foot. I offered a quick hug and a quicker goodbye. Ten minutes later, my son asked for help fixing a science project.

Tape and cardboard were everywhere. I forced a smile, helped a little, and then escaped to my list, irritated and guilty at the same time. In the car, a memory of Jesus came to me. He was on the way to help a dying girl when a woman touched His robe.

The crowd pressed, the clock ticked, yet He stopped. He made room for the interruption that became a miracle. My pace slowed inside. I prayed one sentence, Jesus, teach me to see the person in front of me.

I tried again. When I returned home, I texted my neighbor, Come back if you are free. We sat at the table with those bright lemons between us. She cried.

I listened. We prayed. No fireworks, but the air felt softer. Later, I gave my son my full attention for fifteen minutes.

We tested ramp angles and laughed when the car flew off the table. He beamed like I had handed him the moon. I learned a simple rhythm that day. Build margin.

I now leave ten minutes between tasks so people do not feel like problems. I practice the pause. When interrupted, I take a slow breath, ask, What does love look like right now, and respond from peace, not panic. I also name my limits.

If I cannot engage, I say, I want to give this my full attention at two o'clock. Can we talk then. The point is not to say yes to everything. The point is to say yes to the right person at the right moment, like Jesus did.

Interruptions often carry hidden gifts. A chance to comfort. A chance to teach. A chance to be taught.

When I welcomed them, I found God waiting there.

Prayer

Jesus, slow me to see the person in front of me. Give me a calm center, generous eyes, and wise boundaries. Let my pauses become space for Your work. Help me notice needs and respond with love, even when my schedule feels tight. Amen.

A Moment with God

Who is my likely interruption today, and how will I welcome her?

Day 28: The Complaint Swap

"Do everything without grumbling or arguing, so that you may become blameless and pure, shining among them like stars." Philippians 2:14–15

I did not think I was a complainer. I was just honest about the traffic, the dishes, the weather, the workload, the group chat that never ends. Then one evening my daughter said, "Mom, everything okay You sound grumpy." Her words stung because she was right.

My mouth had turned into a leaking faucet, drip after drip of small complaints that dimmed our home. That night I read Philippians and felt a nudge to try an experiment. For one day, every time I complained, I would swap it for three thank yous, out loud. Morning came with a sink full of pans.

I started to mutter, then caught myself. Thank You for hot water. Thank You for food to cook. Thank You for the hands that will eat at this table.

It felt awkward at first, like changing the direction of a river. But the current shifted. At work, a project changed again. I wanted to sigh.

Instead, I whispered, Thank You for a job. Thank You for a team. Thank You for the chance to learn flexibility. In the car, stuck behind a slow driver, I practiced again.

Thank You for a safe trip. Thank You for time to breathe. Thank You for the song on the radio. My shoulders dropped.

My jaw unclenched. The day grew brighter, not because my circumstances changed, but because my focus did. By evening, my family noticed. Jokes replaced jabs.

We ate together without the fog of negativity. Complaints had been stealing energy we needed for joy. The swap did not mean ignoring real problems. It meant starting with gratitude so solutions could grow in clear light.

Paul said gratitude makes us shine. He was right. A grateful spirit is like a porch light in a dark neighborhood. People feel safe around it.

Now I keep a sticky note on the fridge that says, Swap it. When a complaint rises, I trade it for three thanks. Some days I have to do it a dozen times. That is fine.

Every swap sands down a rough edge in my heart. Over time, gratitude becomes my first instinct, and our home glows a little brighter.

Prayer

Father, place thanks where I want to complain. Train my tongue to bless. Give me eyes to spot Your gifts in ordinary moments. Let gratitude soften my tone, lift my home, and point others to You as the source of every good thing. Amen.

A Moment with God

Identify one repeated complaint and write three alternative thank yous.

Day 29: Clear the Clutter

"Let all things be done decently and in order." 1 Corinthians 14:40

The dining table had disappeared. Backpacks, mail, a sweater I kept meaning to return, half a craft project, and a lonely spoon covered the surface. Every time I walked by, I felt crowded inside. I wanted to invite a friend over, but embarrassment kept winning.

I told myself I needed a full day to fix it, which meant it never happened. One afternoon I set a timer for fifteen minutes and chose one spot, just the table. Trash in the bin. Mail sorted.

Backpack hooks cleared. I wiped the wood and set a small vase with two grocery store daisies. Fifteen minutes turned a pile into a welcome. My heart exhaled.

Order is not about perfection. It is about peace and hospitality. I kept going in tiny pockets. One drawer.

The car cup holders. The entryway basket. Each little reset made our home kinder. I created simple systems so the order would last.

A landing zone by the door for keys and bags. A five minute evening sweep with music. One in, one out for toys and clothes. I even set a weekly ten minute paper session so piles could not boss me around.

Something holy happened as surfaces cleared. Conversations lingered because we had a place to sit. Meals felt special again because we could set plates without a scavenger hunt. I invited that friend, and we laughed at the daisies like they were a fancy centerpiece.

Order served our peace and opened the door to people. God cares about order because He cares about hearts. Chaos drains. Simple systems bless.

You do not need matching bins or a weekend makeover. You need a small decision and a timer. Fifteen focused minutes can restore a space and your spirit. When I live this way, I feel ready to say, Come in.

We have room for you.

Prayer

God, help me bless my home with simple order. Show me the next small space to restore. Give me steady hands, patient choices, and joy as I make room for people and peace. Let my home reflect Your welcome and calm. Amen.

A Moment with God

Which small space will I restore for 15 minutes today?

Day 30: From Comparison to Calling

"Let each one test his own work, and then his reason to boast will be in himself alone and not in his neighbor." Galatians 6:4

*I*t started as a quick peek. A friend's post about her vacation. Another friend's promotion. Someone else's spotless kitchen.

Five minutes later, I was measuring my life with their tape. My gratitude shrank. My confidence wilted. I closed the app but kept scrolling in my mind, replaying what I lacked.

Galatians 6:4 spoke straight to the ache. Test your own work. Do your assignment. Stay in your lane.

I grabbed a notebook and wrote two lists. On the left, places I had compared this week. On the right, my actual gifts and responsibilities. My list surprised me.

I am the only mom my kids have. I am the neighbor to the woman next door. I am the steward of my words, my time, my body. God will ask me about those, not about someone else's highlight reel.

I decided to practice a new habit. When comparison knocked, I would answer with calling. I muted a few accounts that stirred envy and followed people who point me to Jesus. I made a tiny daily assignment list titled My Lane.

Pray for my family by name. Write for thirty minutes. Encourage one person with a text or note. Walk outside for ten minutes and say thank You for what I see.

These were simple, but they re-anchored me. That week, instead of scrolling past a need, I used my gift. I baked muffins and left them on a porch. I drafted a paragraph I had avoided and sent it out.

I played catch in the yard instead of comparing yards online. Joy grew, not because I became the best, but because I became faithful. Gratitude focused me on what God had actually placed in my hands. When I run in my lane, I am lighter.

I can cheer others without shrinking myself. God did not make me to be her. He made me to be me, on purpose. Gratitude keeps my eyes on my assignment, and that is where peace lives.

Prayer

Lord, anchor me in my assignment. Free me from comparison. Help me celebrate others while staying faithful to what You placed in my hands. Show me today's work, and fill me with contentment as I do it with You. Amen.

A Moment with God

Where did I compare this week, and what unique gift will I use instead?

Week 7: Trust Through the Waiting

Day 31: Honest Lament

"How long wilt thou forget me, O LORD? forever? how long wilt thou hide thy face from me... But I have trusted in thy mercy; my heart shall rejoice in thy salvation." Psalm 13:1–2, 5–6

I sat in my car after the call, keys still in the ignition, hands shaking. The news was not a final no, but it was another not yet. I felt tired in a way sleep could not touch. My chest was tight, my jaw clenched, and somewhere under it all was a slow burn of anger I did not want to admit.

I had prayed. I had fasted. I had told myself to stay positive. Yet the ache stayed.

That Sunday, I tried to sing in church and nothing came out. The words on the screen looked like a language I could not speak. I felt guilty about that. Good Christians are grateful, I told myself.

Grateful people do not cry in the second row. Then Psalm 13 showed up in my reading. David does not hide his pain. He asks questions I was afraid to say out loud.

How long, Lord. Are You listening. Do You see me. He does not rush past the ache.

He pours it out with raw honesty, and somehow, that psalm ends with singing. Not because the problem is solved, but because trust has been named alongside sorrow. So I tried it. I wrote a prayer that sounded more like a storm than a poem.

I wrote the real words. I told God I felt forgotten. I told Him I was tired of waiting rooms and polite updates and the hollow feeling after hopeful messages fade. I told Him I wanted to quit hoping so it would hurt less.

And then, in the same breath, I wrote the trust I still had. Not a shiny trust. A thin thread. I remembered small mercies.

The friend who texted right when the tears started. The verse that found me when I was not looking. The way God had held me in other dark nights. I let both live on the same page, grief and gratitude, like two hands reaching for the same Father.

Something loosened. The situation did not change, but my posture did. I was not faking praise. I was learning a deeper kind.

Gratitude did not skip sorrow. It walked through it with God. The next Sunday, my voice was still fragile, but I could whisper. That whisper felt

like worship.

Prayer

God, I bring my grief and my trust. Hold both. Amen.

A Moment with God

What loss do I need to name before I can give thanks?

Day 32: Unanswered Prayers

"Although the fig tree shall not blossom... yet I will rejoice in the LORD, I will joy in the God of my salvation. The LORD God is my strength." Habakkuk 3:17–19

I kept a spreadsheet of prayers. Dates, details, little checkboxes waiting for a yes. Weeks turned into months of sending resumes, making calls, and praying with hopeful energy that slowly thinned. The inbox stayed quiet.

Savings stretched. Pride cracked. I started wondering if I had misheard God or if I was being punished. I did not say that out loud, but the thought sat heavy.

One morning, I read Habakkuk and felt like he had been reading my email. Fields empty. Vines bare. Shelves thin.

He does not deny the lack. He names it line by line. Then he plants his feet on something that does not shift. Yet I will rejoice in the Lord.

Not in the result. In the Lord. Joy, not as a mood swing, but as an act of trust in God's character when outcomes are thin. So I made a new list.

Not of requests, but of who God is. Faithful in my past. Wise when my plans were not. Near to the brokenhearted.

Provider, even when provision looked different than my idea of success. I began to say thank You for Your strength, not mine. Thank You for Your timing, not my schedule. The checkboxes did not fill overnight.

But my anxiety loosened its grip. I also practiced stubborn joy. Not loud. More like a steady flame.

I took a walk and sang softly, even when I did not feel it. I cooked a simple meal and thanked God for the taste of warm bread and the roof over our heads. I sent a note to encourage someone else who was waiting, because joy grows when it is shared. Small habits lifted my eyes from the empty figs to the God who makes feet steady on high places.

The job came later, in a way I did not predict. By then, the deepest gift had already arrived. I had learned where to stand when results are thin. On God's character.

Prayer

Lord, be my strength in the "not yet." Amen.

A Moment with God

Where will I practice stubborn joy this week?

Day 33: Small Beauty

"For who hath despised the day of small things?" Zechariah 4:10

I bought a tiny packet of basil seeds on a whim. The balcony box looked silly with its neat rows of dirt and no green. Every morning I watered and saw nothing. After a week, I almost gave up.

Then one day, I leaned in and spotted it. One speck of green, like a freckle on the soil. I laughed out loud. It was so small I could have missed it.

That summer was crowded with slow battles. Healing that took longer than planned. A relationship that needed careful words. Bills that required creative math.

I wanted big breakthroughs, but what I got were tiny shoots. A kind email. A pain-free hour. A five-minute conversation that did not spiral.

I kept thinking, This is not enough. Then Zechariah's question nudged me. Who despises the day of small things. God does not.

So I started watching for small beauty the way I watched that planter. Morning light striping the kitchen floor. The first sip of hot coffee. A child's belly laugh in the grocery aisle.

A song on the radio that landed like rain. Noticing did not make the hard vanish, but it changed the air in the room. Gratitude grew in little sips. I felt my shoulders drop.

I smiled without forcing it. Small beginnings carry quiet power. The first apology opens the way to real repair. The first evening walk becomes strength I did not know I had.

The early savings deposit becomes a habit that steadies a family. God often builds with small bricks. Jesus fed thousands with a lunch that looked laughably small. The Spirit writes big stories with tiny lines.

On the balcony, the basil did not burst overnight. It thickened day by day until the box was fragrant and full. I snipped a handful and stirred it into pasta. It tasted like summer and patience.

I whispered thanks. Not for a flashy miracle, but for a God who delights to begin small and stay close.

Prayer

Father, open my eyes to hidden beauty today. Amen.

A Moment with God

Write five small beauties you notice right now.

Day 34: Purpose in Pain

"And we know that all things work together for good to them that love God."
Romans 8:28

After the accident, stairs felt like mountains. Physical therapy was a room full of grit. Stretch, hold, breathe, try again. I hated the mirror that showed my slow progress.

I wanted my old speed back. I wanted the pain to mean something, or at least to end. People tried to help with easy lines. I knew they meant well, but fast words felt like salt.

What steadied me was not a slogan. It was the patient presence of God and a promise that did not erase pain, but refused to waste it. Romans 8:28 is not a sticker you slap on a wound. It is a deep truth about a Redeemer who can weave even tangled threads into good for those who love Him.

In therapy I met Mara. She was quiet and scared to move. I recognized her look. One day I sat beside her between sets and said, I know this is hard.

She nodded and tears fell. We began talking each week. We swapped playlists. We prayed before we started.

The room did not get easier, but it grew kinder. I realized my pain was forming something in me that comfort could not. Patience. Compassion.

Strength that did not brag. I still prayed for healing, and God answered in inches. I learned to celebrate inches. I learned to ask, How might God use this season to make me more like Jesus.

Not how fast will You end it, but who will You make me through it. I would not call the injury good. It was not. But God was near and at work in it.

Out of that season came a ministry of checking in on others in recovery. A simple text, a meal on a doorstep, a ride to an appointment. Small threads, woven into good. I walk more freely now.

When I take the stairs two at a time, I remember the room that shaped me. Pain was not the final word. God was.

Prayer

Redeemer, weave my pain into Your good purposes. Amen.

A Moment with God

How might God be forming me through this hardship?

Day 35: Steady Hope

"We glory in tribulations also: knowing that tribulation worketh patience... and hope maketh not ashamed; because the love of God is shed abroad in our hearts by the Holy Ghost." Romans 5:3–5

I started running to clear my head. The first day, I barely made it to the corner. My lungs burned, and my cheeks were hot with more than sweat. I felt foolish.

The next day, I tried again. Two houses farther. Then a block. Progress was so small it felt invisible.

Part of me wanted to quit and settle back onto the couch. Romans 5 reframed the whole thing for me. Endurance is not glamorous. It is formed in the pressure cooker.

Suffering produces endurance, and endurance produces character, and character produces hope that does not shame us. Not because we are impressive, but because the Spirit pours God's love into our hearts while we wait and work. So I looked for signs of endurance I could thank God for right now. Lacing up when I did not feel like it.

Choosing water over soda. Turning off the show to sleep. Texting a friend to pray when the old thoughts crept in. Each was small, but each was real.

I began to say, Thank You, Spirit, for love that meets me mid-lap. Thank You for strength I did not have last month. Thank You for a hope that is not a guess, but a gift. Life gave me harder courses than sidewalks.

A long medical test cycle. A tense family situation that did not resolve overnight. I noticed the same muscles working. Keep showing up.

Keep telling the truth. Keep praying when answers are slow. The Holy Spirit did what He promised. He kept my heart from hardening, and He kept hope alive without making me pretend.

Tears came, but so did courage. One morning I finished a 5K at a slow but steady pace. There was no crowd, just a sunrise and a quiet yes inside me. Hope is not ashamed to grow slowly.

It stands up straighter because God's love holds it from within.

Prayer

Spirit, pour love into my heart as I wait. Amen.

A Moment with God

What sign of endurance can I thank God for today?

Week 8: Overflow to Others

Day 36: Blessed to Bless

"I will make you into a great nation, and I will bless you; I will make your name great, and you will be a blessing." (Genesis 12:2)

It happened in the cereal aisle. A mom with a toddler on her hip and a baby in the cart stared at the prices, lips pressed tight. I had come for oat milk and a quick exit. I almost walked past.

Then I remembered this simple truth that had been sitting in my chest all week: God does not pour blessings into us so we can hoard them. He pours so we overflow. I felt the nudge. Pay for her groceries.

My stomach flipped. What if she thinks I am strange? What if I cannot cover it all? What if it is awkward?

I took a breath and prayed under it. Lord, You blessed me. Make me brave enough to be a blessing. At the register, I stepped forward and said, "Can I cover this today?"

Her eyes filled. She whispered, "You have no idea." The total was less than I feared. The joy was more than I expected.

I walked out lighter than my bag. I wanted to run back and do it again. But generosity is not always about money. Later that day, I texted a friend who had gone quiet.

I wrote three sentences of gratitude for her friendship and two ways I see God in her. She responded with a voice note, crying happy tears. Words are free, but they are not cheap. They carry weight when they are born from thanks.

The next morning, I made a small plan. I cleaned out a closet and set aside a box for a single mom down the street. I placed a sticky note on my debit card that says, "Bless fund." I set a calendar reminder called "Overflow hour" for Saturdays, a standing date to look for one need close to me.

Gratitude had sharpened my eyes. I started seeing needs I had skimmed past before, like flowers hiding in plain sight. Here is the breakthrough I keep relearning: gratitude is not a lake, it is a river. When I remember how God has carried me, provided for me, forgiven me, and surprised me, my heart loosens its fist.

I stop asking, "What if I run out?" and start asking, "Who can I pour into?" Abraham was blessed to be a blessing. So are we. The more I give, the more room I make for God to fill again.

Prayer

God, You have poured kindness into my life. Let gratitude move my hands and feet. Show me a need near me, and give me courage to meet it with joy, not fear. Make me a channel of Your generosity so someone tastes Your love today, in real, practical ways. Amen.

A Moment with God

Who will I bless and how within 48 hours?

Day 37: Hospitality at Any Size

"Share with the Lord's people who are in need. Practice hospitality." (Romans 12:13)

ur apartment is small. The table wobbles if you lean on the edge. The couch has a mysterious stain that no cleaner has conquered. For years I told myself, When we have a bigger place, then I will invite people.

Meanwhile, the years kept passing and the table stayed empty. Then my neighbor, Mrs. Lopez, lost her husband. I stood at my sink watching her shuffle across the parking lot with two grocery bags and a sagging spirit. The verse popped into my head like a gentle knock.

Share. Practice. Not perfection. Presence.

I texted her and wrote, "Soup tonight if you are up for it." She replied with a heart. I stared at my mismatched bowls and felt heat crawl up my neck. What if she sees the stain on the couch?

What if the soup is bland? What if I run out of conversation? She arrived in a soft sweater that smelled like lavender. We sat at the wobbly table.

I apologized for the mess. She waved her hand. "I came for company, not a showroom." We ate simple potato soup, crusty bread, and store cookies on a chipped plate.

She talked about her husband and the way he used to hum in the morning. I told her my favorite story about how God met me during a lonely season. We laughed. We cried.

After she left, the apartment felt bigger, like the walls had pushed back to make room for peace. That night I wrote a new definition of hospitality in my journal. Hospitality is the art of making room for someone's heart. It is a warm hello, a chair, a listening ear, and maybe a hot drink.

It can happen at a park, on a porch, or over a phone call. It can be a picnic blanket with peanut butter sandwiches. It can be a pot of tea and ten minutes of quiet presence. The breakthrough was simple.

Gratitude turns my space into a sanctuary. When I thank God for what I have, I stop apologizing for what I do not. I stop waiting for the perfect set up and start opening the door I already own. The joy was not in the menu.

It was in the welcome.

Prayer

Lord, turn my home and heart into warm spaces where people breathe easier. Help me trade perfection for presence. Give me eyes to notice who needs a chair, a mug, a listening ear. Fill my table with Your peace and simple joy, starting this week today and always, please. Amen.

A Moment with God

Plan one simple act of hospitality this week.

Day 38: Speaking Life

"The tongue has the power of life and death." (Proverbs 18:21)

It was a long day and my teenager dropped a glass. It shattered into glittering pieces. I felt the words rising, sharp and fast. Why can't you be more careful?

I could see how this could go. I say it. He shuts down. We both walk away heavy.

Something held me. I remembered the verse and my grandmother's voice, "Child, words are seeds." I thought about the seeds I had planted lately. Were they growing joy or choking it?

I took a deep breath and said, "Hey, I know you did not mean to. Are you okay?" He nodded, surprised. We cleaned up together.

While we swept, he told me about a rough moment at school. The broken glass turned into an open door. Later that night, he texted me a picture of the clean kitchen with a thumbs up. My heart softened.

One held-back sentence made space for connection. It kept happening. At work, a coworker presented an idea that needed work. I was ready to slice it to pieces with smart words.

Instead, I asked a question, praised what was strong, and offered one clear improvement. The meeting ended with energy instead of defense. I walked out thinking, Life or death. Build or break.

Bless or drain. I get to choose the crop by choosing the seeds. Here is the practice that is changing me. Before I speak, I picture a small gate at my lips.

I ask three quick questions at the gate. Is it true? Is it kind? Is it helpful right now?

If I cannot say yes to at least two, I wait. That tiny pause is a miracle maker. The breakthrough is both humbling and exciting. Gratitude tunes my ear to what God is doing, and then my words join the music.

Thankful people tend to speak life. They notice good and name it. They correct with hope instead of shame. They choose silence when a moment needs air.

I am not perfect at this. But the more I practice, the more my home feels lighter, my work calmer, and my heart steadier. Words build worlds. I want mine to look like light.

Prayer

Father, train my tongue to carry life. Put a holy pause between my feelings and my words. Let encouragement rise first. Nudge me when silence is wiser. Use my mouth to plant hope, truth, and joy in weary hearts, beginning with my own today. In Jesus' name I pray. Amen.

A Moment with God

Who needs a life-giving word from me today?

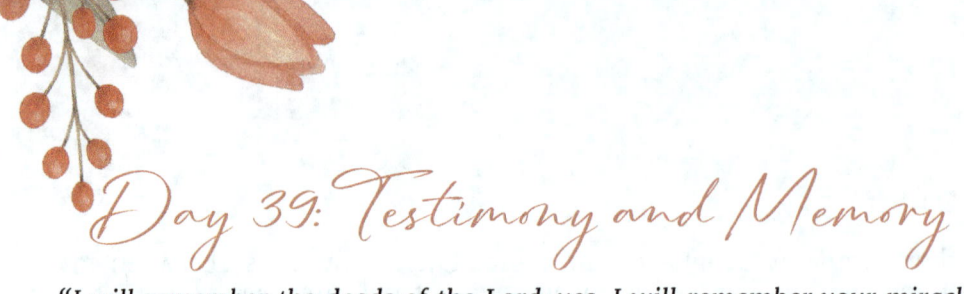

Day 39: Testimony and Memory

"I will remember the deeds of the Lord; yes, I will remember your miracles of long ago. I will consider all your works and meditate on all your mighty deeds." (Psalm 77:11–12)

Two months ago, I hit a dry patch. Prayers felt thin. Bible pages looked like paper instead of bread. I wondered if I had made up God's nearness.

One night I pulled an old shoebox from the closet and dumped out a tangle of note cards, photos, and ticket stubs. It was messy and holy. There was the picture of the tiny apartment we almost lost. On the back I had written, "Rent paid at the last minute by a surprise bonus."

There was the hospital bracelet from the night my daughter could not catch her breath. Scribbled on a napkin was the doctor's phrase I will never forget, "Clear lungs. You can go home." There was a wrinkled receipt from a gas station where a stranger paid for my tank and said, "God told me to."

I sat on the carpet and cried quiet tears. My living room turned into a sanctuary as memory became testimony. I was not just reading about God's faithfulness. I was staring at it in colors and ink.

Faith started to rise again, like a bird that had been resting on the ground. The next day I told my friend at coffee, "I forgot how much God has carried me." She smiled and said, "Say it out loud more. Someone needs that story."

So I did. I told my small group about the hospital bracelet. I texted my cousin the rent story. Every time I spoke, courage grew in me and in them.

Remembered works fuel future faith. Testimony is memory set on fire. Now I keep a "God file" on my phone and a small basket on my shelf. I drop in a sticky note when prayers are answered.

I keep one sentence summaries with dates. On Sundays, I pick one and thank God by name. When my faith feels thin, I read them out loud until my heart catches up. The breakthrough is this.

Gratitude needs memory. Memory needs telling. When I remember and tell, the fog lifts and the path ahead does not feel so dark. He was faithful then.

He will be faithful now.

Prayer

Lord, weave my memories into a witness. Bring to mind Your rescues, guidance, and quiet gifts. Teach me to tell the story simply and boldly so someone else finds courage. Help me stack new stones of remembrance this week through worship, journaling, and sharing. Make it clear for others. Amen.

A Moment with God

Write one paragraph of testimony from these weeks.

Day 40: Vision for the Next Forty

"Where there is no vision, the people perish." (Proverbs 29:18)

We reached day forty and I took a slow walk at the park. The lake was glassy, reflecting cotton clouds and a sky that looked freshly washed. I thought about these weeks. The groceries paid for.

The soup shared. The words held back and the words given. The memories told. A quiet joy hummed under my ribs.

Gratitude had been doing construction inside me, building a steadier core. At a picnic table, I opened my journal and wrote a simple sentence. I want a gentle, clear vision for the next forty days. Not a sprint.

A steady pace that keeps me outward, thankful, and available. Vision is not a Pinterest board. It is a path with small steps that keep me close to God and useful to people. I sketched three small circles, like stepping stones on a trail, and asked God to fill them.

I sensed this: First, start days with wonder. One minute of thanks before my feet hit the floor. Name three gifts out loud.

Sun through the blinds. Warm coffee. New mercies. Second, practice weekly overflow.

Choose one person to bless every week in a concrete way. A meal, a ride, a note, a bill covered, a prayer spoken face to face. Third, keep a life giving tongue. Set a phone reminder at noon that says, "Speak life."

Send one encouraging text. Name one good thing to someone near me. Apologize fast when I miss it. I added two guardrails to protect the vision.

Rest on purpose every week so I do not run dry. Listen for God before I plan my next thing. Vision without listening becomes noise. Vision with gratitude becomes a song.

Here is what settled in my heart. Gratitude does not just color the past. It shapes the future. It sounds like this: I will walk slower, look closer, and give freer because God is with me.

I do not need a grand platform. I need a clear path and a soft heart. Forty days from now, I want to look back and see a trail of simple love.

Prayer

God, shape a gentle, sturdy vision for the next forty days and beyond.

Let gratitude lead every plan. Set my pace by Your presence. Prune what distracts. Grow what brings life. Make my steps faithful, creative, and joyful in the small and the large. Hold me close each day. Amen.

A Moment with God

Draft a simple "Rule of Life" with three gratitude habits to continue.

Your feedback is a true blessing!

If this book has encouraged you or helped you feel less alone, would you leave a quick review?

Even one sentence makes a huge difference and takes just a minute. As a small author, your feedback not only lifts my heart... It also helps other women of faith find the support and hope they need.

Thank you for being part of this journey!

Scan this QR code with your phone to go to the review page

Or

Go to your orders, find the book and click

"Write a product review"

Thank you <3

Receive and spread truth

ou've reached the end of this devotional, but this is not the end of your journey. Gratitude is not something you finish; it is something you carry. It grows quietly, showing up in how you speak with kindness, how you wait with patience, and how you notice small blessings in your everyday life.

The beauty of gratitude is that you can return to it again and again. Revisit your favorite weeks. Pray the prayers that gave you strength. Take the simple steps once more. God's Word will always meet you right where you are.

If this book has helped you, it would mean so much if you'd leave a review. I read every single one, and your words help other women find the support they need on their own journey.

"Therefore encourage one another and build each other up, just as in fact you are doing."
— 1 Thessalonians 5:11

Sometimes the people in our lives need these tools too, or simply want to understand you better. You can write the names of people you can gift this book to, to enhance their lives and yours:

....
....
....
....
....

If you want more beautiful devotionals like this, you can go to my author page "Esther Ellison" on amazon and find them.

Thank you for letting me walk with you through this season. May this not be the end, but the beginning of a new rhythm of grace in your life.

With love and gratitude,

Esther <3

www.ingramcontent.com/pod-product-compliance
Lightning Source LLC
Chambersburg PA
CBHW071538120626
46550CB00006B/2495